Praise for **Ready for Bed!** and the ParentSmart/KidHappy™ Series:

"Stacey Kaye has created a must-have series that will make life easier for parents and their children. In a delightfully entertaining way, kids will learn from a very early age skills to resolve typical, everyday struggles—skills they will take with them for the rest of their lives."

—**Myrna B. Shure, Ph.D.**, author of *Raising a Thinking Child* and *Thinking Parent, Thinking Child*

"These books present important concepts to parents and children. They can help children learn to be aware of feelings and to engage in problem solving, key components of emotional intelligence. The explanation of these concepts at the end of the book is also important for parents to be able to generalize these skills to other areas of the child's life."

—**Steven Tobias, Psy.D.**, coauthor of *Emotionally Intelligent Parenting*

"Through storytelling and role-modeling, each page provides a thoughtful approach to tackling this important daily routine."

—**Donna Erickson**, host of award-winning *Donna's Day* on public television, author of *Donna Erickson's Fabulous Funstuff for Families,* and syndicated newspaper columnist

"ParentSmart/KidHappy is for any family looking for ways to get through those all-too-common everyday struggles. Reading these realistic stories together, kids and parents learn positive, hassle-free solutions to those universal battles."

—**Nancy Samalin, M.S.**, lecturer and best-selling author of *Loving Without Spoiling: And 100 Other Timeless Tips for Raising Terrific Kids*

"ParentSmart/KidHappy is a lifesaver for any stressed parent (do you know one who isn't?) who wants to ease daily battles and raise an emotionally healthy child."

—**Dr. Michele Borba**, author of *No More Misbehavin'* and *Parents Do Make a Difference*

Ready for Bed!

A Tale of Cleaning Up, Tucking In, and Hardly Any Complaining

by Stacey R. Kaye

illustrated by Elizabeth O. Dulemba

edited by Eric Braun

free spirit

PUBLISHING®

To Steven, Audrey, and Margo.
—S.K.

For Kate, Brady, Quinn, Olivia, Hugh, and Maddie.
—Cousin e

Acknowledgments

Thank you to Scott Harman, MSW, LICSW, and Michele Fallon, LICSW, for reading drafts of the manuscript and providing valuable feedback.

Library of Congress Cataloging-in-Publication Data
Kaye, Stacey R.
   Ready for bed! : a tale of cleaning up, tucking in, and hardly any complaining / by Stacey R. Kaye ; illustrated by Elizabeth O. Dulemba.
      p. cm.
   ISBN-13: 978-1-57542-269-5
   ISBN-10: 1-57542-269-7
   1. Bedtime—Juvenile literature. 2. Night. I. Dulemba, Elizabeth O. II. Title.
   HQ784.B43K39 2007
   649'.6—dc22
                                                            2008031364

Cover and interior design by Marieka Heinlen and Michelle Lee

10 9 8 7 6 5 4 3 2
Printed in China
P17201208

Free Spirit Publishing Inc.
217 Fifth Avenue North, Suite 200
Minneapolis, MN 55401-1299
(612) 338-2068
help4kids@freespirit.com
www.freespirit.com

Grown-ups:

The language of positive parenting
in this book is color-coded.

Blue words offer choices.
Green words validate feelings.
Red words encourage.

Learn more about these techniques
at the end of the book.

Mommy says it's time for bed, but Marco isn't ready.
"I don't *want* to go to bed!"

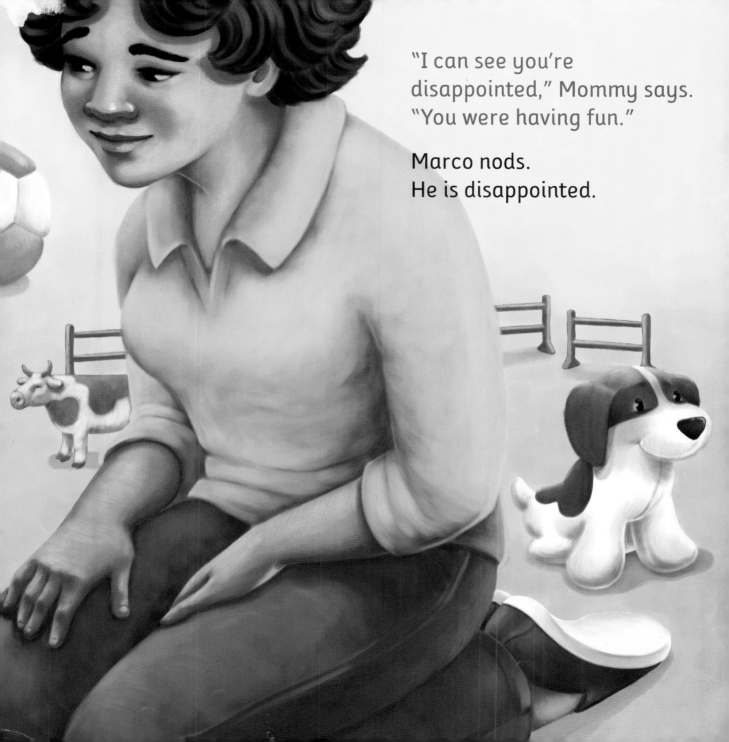

"I can see you're disappointed," Mommy says. "You were having fun."

Marco nods.
He is disappointed.

"Do you want to choose how we get ready tonight?"

"Yeah!" Marco says.

...vrooooooo

"Would you like to swim like a fish or fly like an airplane to the bathtub? You choose."

Marco jumps up. "Airplane!"

oooooooom

"Flight 123 coming in for a landing—all clear!" Mommy says.

"I want bubbles in the bath!" Marco says. "I mean, bubbles, please!"

"You remembered your manners! Here come the bubbles."

Mommy asks, "Do you want to wash your hair or your body first? You choose."

Marco makes a joke when he points to his hair and answers, "Body!"

Mommy gives a little tickle as she washes under his arm.

"All clean," Mommy says. "Time to get out of the bath."

"Noooooooooooooooooo!" Marco whines.

"You really like playing in the tub. It's hard to stop playing, isn't it?"

"Yes," Marco says, calming down.
Mommy always tries to understand how he feels.

"Let's play for five more minutes," she says.
"Here comes another boat."

"Yay!" squeals Marco.

Marco is clean and dry.

"Would you like to wear your crocodile jammies or your blue stripeys?" Mommy asks.

Marco shivers under his towel. "Crocodiles, p-p-puh-lease."

"Aw, my little croc is cold. Better slip on these toasty-cuddly jammies."

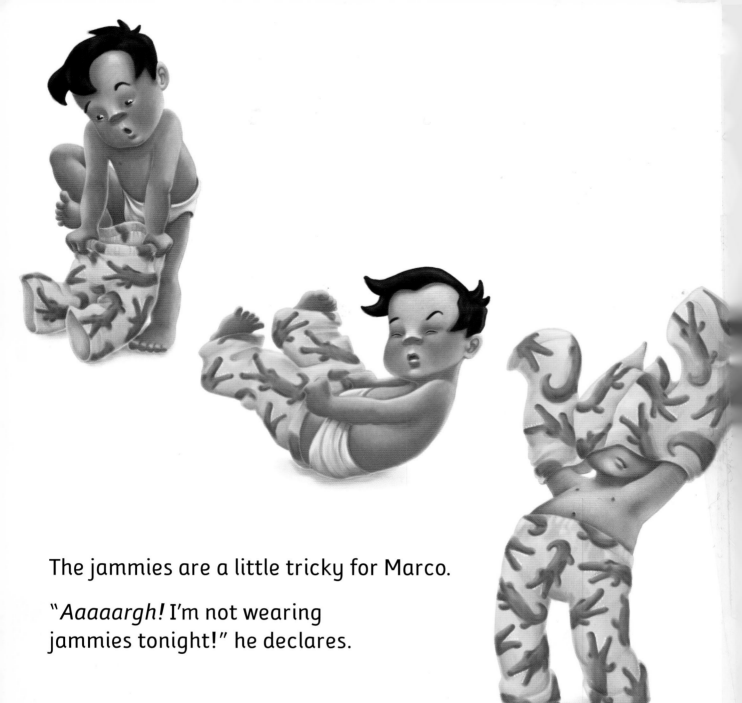

The jammies are a little tricky for Marco.

"*Aaaaargh!* I'm not wearing
jammies tonight!" he declares.

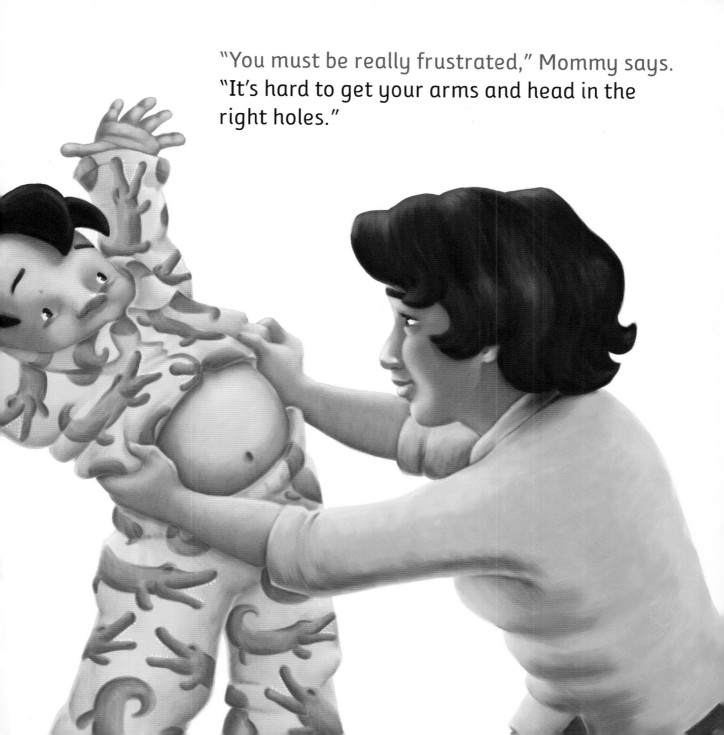

"You must be really frustrated," Mommy says. "It's hard to get your arms and head in the right holes."

"Time to brush your chompers," Mommy says. "Would you like to brush first, or should I take my turn brushing them first?"

"You first," Marco says. "But watch out! I am a very hungry crocodile! *Chomp, chomp.*"

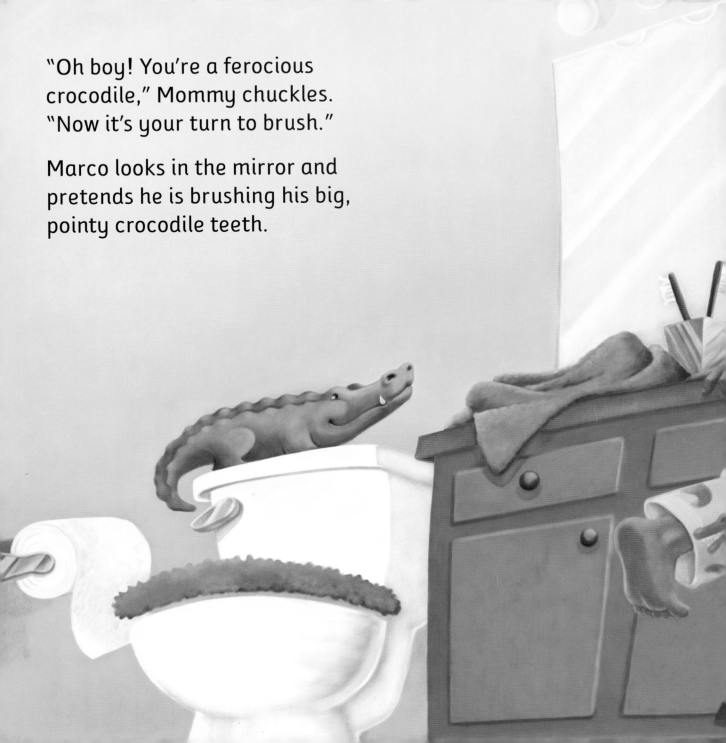

"Oh boy! You're a ferocious crocodile," Mommy chuckles. "Now it's your turn to brush."

Marco looks in the mirror and pretends he is brushing his big, pointy crocodile teeth.

"Ta-Dah! You worked hard to get your teeth clean. You even brushed your teeth all the way in the back."

"Marco, you made getting ready for bed so much fun," Mommy says. "We worked so well together we have time for an extra story."

"All right!" Marco says.

"What did you like best about getting ready for bed tonight?"

"Being a crocodile," Marco says. "*Chomp chomp!*"

"Good night, Mommy!"

"Good night, Marco.
I love you!"

Encouraging Cooperation
And Raising Confident, Emotionally Intelligent Children

As most parents and caregivers of preschool-age children know, transitions such as bedtime can be very frustrating—especially when we're tired! Many of us have resorted to threatening timeouts, taking away a favorite toy or book, or bribing with rewards. While these techniques may seem natural, and may even get short-term results, they're probably not going to prevent the same struggle from arising again tomorrow night. And none of these approaches teaches our kids to think for themselves or acknowledges that their feelings are important.

Of course, kids' feelings *are* important, even when they feel frustrated or mad—or when they just feel like staying up! Research shows that kids who believe the adults in their lives respect them and think they are important are more likely to cooperate during transitions. Those kids are *also* more likely to grow in self-esteem, independence, and emotional intelligence.

The term "emotional intelligence" refers to our ability to recognize emotions in ourselves and others and to manage our emotions. Experts such as Daniel Goleman, who has written several books on the subject, consider emotional intelligence a key to developing strong relationships, an optimistic outlook, self-confidence, and general happiness.

The important thing is to work *with* kids rather than manipulating them (with rewards or other methods). In this way, we can help them develop their emotional intelligence while we encourage them to cooperate during transitions. No book can tell you exactly what to say to the children in your life, but the following are basic guidelines recommended by psychologists and parenting experts.

Validate Feelings

Children who know that feelings are normal and feelings have names have an easier time managing and expressing them appropriately. Children who learn to recognize and manage their feelings also learn to have empathy for other people's feelings. In turn, these skills help kids improve social skills and do better in school.

It's important to acknowledge children's feelings even if you can't accommodate them. Letting kids know you understand how they feel shows that you think they and their feelings are important. A child who feels important is more likely to cooperate, have high self-esteem, and develop positive emotional health.

To help kids learn about emotions, talk with them about their feelings, your feelings, and the feelings of others. Recognize feelings, name them, and make it clear that all feelings are acceptable. It's fine, for example, to be disappointed that it's time for bed. It's natural. However, not all ways of *showing* feelings are acceptable. You might say, "It's okay to feel disappointed. Hitting is not okay."

Parents and caregivers can set an example. If you feel tired, frustrated, proud, silly—talk about it. Show your child that no matter how you feel you can still be fair, considerate, and loving. When reading books, ask your child how a character in the story might be feeling. Encourage your child to think about the feelings of others.

Understanding a child's point of view is more important than fixing the problem. Be present, help label the feelings, be patient, and demonstrate acceptance (reserve judgment).

- You really miss Mommy, don't you? I'm sorry she's not home now. I miss her, too.
- I would feel the same way.
- Ouch! That must really hurt.
- It sounds like you are really angry.
- It can be disappointing when your friend won't share.

In the main part of this book, look for dialogue in green for other examples of validating feelings.

Offer Choices

Kids often feel powerless when grown-ups tell them what to do and what not to do. As a result, they may seek power by resisting you. Instead of commanding kids to do something, try offering a choice and watch them embrace the opportunity to feel in control of the situation. Giving kids choices empowers children and has several benefits. It takes the air out of power struggles so you can get things done without a battle. And the long-term benefits are even better. Children who are regularly given choices are more independent, more skilled at making decisions, and more aware of the relationship between their decisions and possible outcomes. Finally, and maybe most important, having choices makes kids feel good.

Giving up some power doesn't mean you stop being the adult. It means you look for parts of a situation that you are willing to let the child control. Be sure to offer appropriate choices. Kids aren't mature enough to choose their own bedtime, for example. Offer specific options: "Would you like to wear the red shirt or the blue one?" Limit options to two or three for preschoolers.

Sometimes a tired child may seem overwhelmed by choices, or resist them altogether. When that happens, it's important for the adult to step in: "It looks like it's hard to choose right now. I'll decide this time and you can choose next time."

More examples:

- Would you like to take a bath or a shower?
- Which would you like to clean up first, the checkers game or this princess puzzle?
- Would you like me to help you tie your shoes or do you want to tie them yourself?
- Would you like to take teddy or bunny along for the car ride?

Look for dialogue in blue for other examples of offering choices.

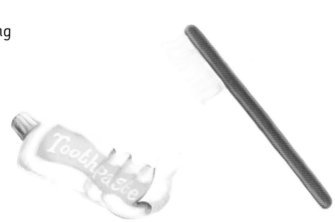

Give Encouragement

Let kids know you are proud of their efforts by offering specific words of encouragement. Instead of saying simply, "Good job!" notice and comment on what the child has done. "You put your crayons away before I even asked you to," or "You ate all your broccoli." Kids are much more likely to believe and react to specific encouragement.

Experts in child development point out that encouragement is different from praise. Praise—saying things like "Good job" or "Good boy"—conditions children to seek adults' approval rather than doing things for their own satisfaction. Praise focuses on the results of their efforts, assigns value to the results, and teaches kids they are only acceptable to you when they do well at things. Encouragement, on the other hand, focuses on their efforts and lets them know you love them and think they are important *no matter how well they perform*. For example, "You remembered to say please" encourages, whereas "Good job remembering your manners" praises.

Effective encouragement is also sincere. Here are some examples:

- You showed a lot of responsibility when you picked up your toys.
- Wow! You figured it out all by yourself.
- How did you do that? *or* Tell me how you did that!
- I can see why you are so proud.

Nonverbal gestures of encouragement also go a long way!
- a smile
- a pat on the shoulder or back
- a high five
- a hug

Look for dialogue in red for other examples of encouragement.

If the suggestions in this book feel unnatural or uncomfortable at first, try not to be intimidated! The mother in this story uses many techniques in a short period of time in order to provide plenty of examples of the language of positive parenting. As a first step, try using the technique that seems most natural and comfortable for you. Repeated use over time will make the language more comfortable and lead to improved cooperation. Don't be discouraged if you don't see immediate changes in your family. It can take time, but it's worth it!

About the Author

Stacey R. Kaye, MMR, is the mother of two young children and a self-described "Parenting Lecture Groupie." As her first daughter grew into a feisty toddler, Stacey searched for a language she could use to discourage tantrums and meltdowns while at the same time encouraging her daughter to explore, grow confidence, and gain emotional intelligence. Dozens of parenting tomes, lectures, and courses provided great theory, but not the language. That's when Stacey began writing ParentSmart/KidHappy books.

To learn more positive parenting tips and discover other ParentSmart/KidHappy titles, visit **www.ParentSmartKidHappy.com**.

About the Illustrator

Award winning author/illustrator **Elizabeth O. Dulemba** was beamed to this planet with a pencil in her hand. Once she stopped chewing on it, she began to write and draw. She received her Bachelor of Fine Arts in Graphic Design from the University of Georgia and in 2001 began illustrating children's books. She now has several titles to her credit including the bilingual *Paco and the Giant Chile Plant* and *The Prince's Diary*, which Book Sense named the No. 1 Valentine's Day Pick of 2006. She enjoys sharing her passion for children's books at schools and events.

Elizabeth lives in Atlanta with her husband Stan, two big dogs, and a tiny cat who rules them all. Visit her Web site to learn more and download free coloring pages: **www.dulemba.com**.

Other Great Books from Free Spirit

Also in the ParentSmart/KidHappy™ Series

Ready for the Day!
A Tale of Teamwork and Toast, and Hardly Any Foot-Dragging
by Stacey R. Kaye, MMR, illustrated by Elizabeth O. Dulemba
Getting a preschooler out the door in the morning can be a frustrating battle of wills complete with crying and complaining—by parents and kids alike. *Ready for the Day!* offers a healthy, lasting solution. Share this kid-friendly storybook with your child and you'll both learn a new, positive way to get ready without stress. Replace the begging, bribing, and brawling with positive parenting. Learn how working with kids in a respectful, give-and-take relationship gets better results and helps kids grow from the inside out. For ages 3–6.
Hardcover; 32 pp.; color illust.; 8" x 8".

Ready to Play!
A Tale of Toys and Friends, and Barely Any Bickering
by Stacey R. Kaye, MMR, illustrated by Elizabeth O. Dulemba
Trouble sharing. Haggles over what to play. Jealousy, hurt feelings—and of course tears when playtime ends. For kids just learning to get along, playtime can be riddled with conflict. *Ready to Play!* offers healthy, lasting ways to help kids cooperate, develop social skills, and have fun. For ages 3–6.
Hardcover; 32 pp.; color illust.; 8" x 8".

Free Spirit's Learning to Get Along® Series

by Cheri J. Meiners, M.Ed.
Help children learn, understand, and practice basic social and emotional skills. Real-life situations, diversity, and concrete examples make these read-aloud books appropriate for childcare settings, schools, and the home. For ages 4–8.
Each book: Paperback; 40 pp.; color illust.; 9" x 9".

SERIES INCLUDES:

- Accept and Value Each Person
- Reach Out and Give
- Share and Take Turns
- Understand and Care
- Listen and Learn

- Be Careful and Stay Safe
- Try and Stick with It
- Know and Follow Rules
- When I Feel Afraid
- Join In and Play

- Talk and Work It Out
- Be Polite and Kind
- Be Honest and Tell the Truth
- Respect and Take Care of Things

From Free Spirit's Best Behavior™ Series

Hands Are Not for Hitting

by Martine Agassi, Ph.D., illustrated by Marieka Heinlen
Little ones learn that violence is never okay, hands can do many good things, and everyone is capable of positive, loving actions.
Paperback for ages 4–7. 40 pp.; color illust.; 9" x 9".
Board book for ages baby–preschool. 24 pp.; color illust.; 7" x 7".

Words Are Not for Hurting

by Elizabeth Verdick, illustrated by Marieka Heinlen
Even very young children can learn that their words affect other people in powerful ways. This book guides them to choose words that are helpful instead of hurtful, and to say "I'm sorry" when hurtful words come out before kids can stop them.
Paperback for ages 4–7. 40 pp.; color illust.; 9" x 9".
Board book for ages baby–preschool. 24 pp.; color illust.; 7" x 7".

free spirit
PUBLISHING®

217 Fifth Avenue North • Suite 200 • Minneapolis, MN 55401 • toll-free 800.735.7323
local 612.338.2068 • fax 612.337.5050 • help4kids@freespirit.com • **www.freespirit.com**

For pricing information, to place an order, or to request a free catalog, contact us.

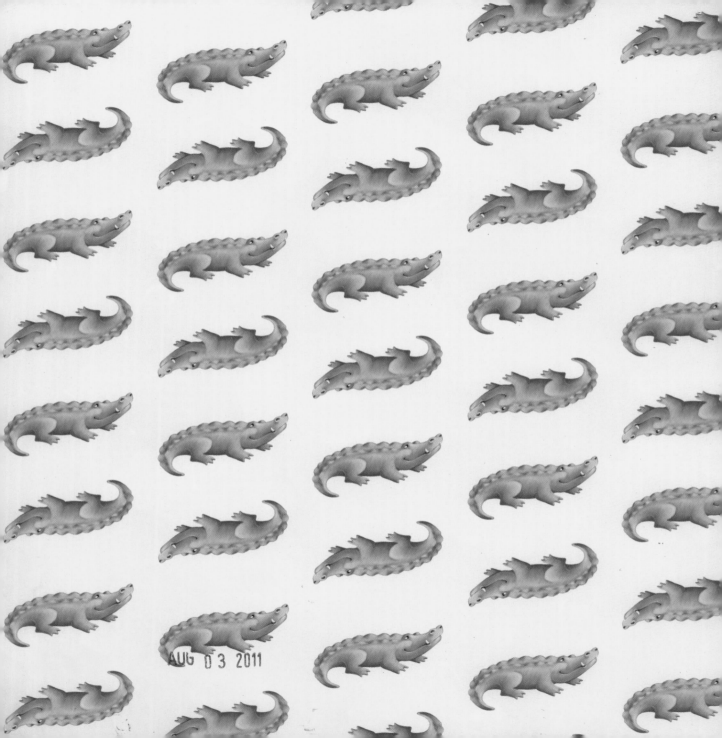